Original title:
Whispers and Waves

Editor: Theodor Taimla
Author: Regiina Rannaveer
ISBN HARDBACK: 978-9916-763-68-1
ISBN PAPERBACK: 978-9916-763-69-8

Tales of the Tide

In the whisper of the early dawn,
Waves compose a timeless song.
Silver tides that rise and fall,
Echoes from an ancient throng.

Footprints fleeting on the strand,
Stories carved in shifting sand.
Memories of a world long gone,
Retold by ocean's gentle hand.

Barnacles and shells ascribe,
Secret codes that winds describe.
Salty tales of mariners brave,
Crafted by a tidal scribe.

Songs of the Surf

On moonlit shores where dreams escape,
Ocean's hymns begin to shape.
Melodies in frothy foam,
Serenades of endless roam.

Storms may roar and thunder loud,
Yet the surf, both vast and proud,
Whispers verses soft and clear,
To those who truly wish to hear.

Crashing waves like cymbal's clash,
Under skies where seabirds dash.
Rhythms born of nature's grace,
In the surf's embrace, wild and vast.

Lull of Liquid Dreams

In the cradle of the night,
Oceans weave a soft delight.
Liquid dreams that ebb and flow,
Cradlesong of undertow.

Moonbeams dance on waves so deep,
Lulling hearts to gentle sleep.
Stars like gems in azure skies,
Watch as slumber softly sighs.

Silent whispers, quiet beams,
Guide us through these liquid dreams.
Restful waters, hushed and wide,
Soothe the soul with cooling tide.

Mysteries Beneath

Below the sea where shadows play,
Mysteries in the deep do lay.
Coral realms and hidden coves,
Secrets kept in underwater groves.

Mermaid tales and sunken ships,
Silent realms where no sound slips.
Treasures lost to time's embrace,
Guarded by the deep's own grace.

Diving through the sapphire veil,
We glimpse a world both old and frail.
Mysteries beneath the waves,
In ocean's depths, where silence saves.

Tidal Whispers

Beneath the moon's soft silver glow,
Waves tell secrets, ebb and flow.
Whispers found in shell and sand,
Stories washed upon the land.

Dancing waves in silent dance,
Rippled whispers, hearts entranced.
In the quiet of the night,
Tides reveal their hidden light.

Foamy crests kiss twilight's shore,
Weaving tales forevermore.
As night folds with gentle sweep,
Tides their whispered secrets keep.

Echoes of Ebb and Flow

A symphony of tides in tune,
Sings beneath the gentle moon.
Ebb and flow, a timeless song,
Nature's voice, both pure and strong.

Ocean's heart beats steady, true,
Blending sky with deepest blue.
Each retreat and each advance,
Forms a dance of circumstance.

Shoreline shifts with measured grace,
Leaving echoes in its place.
Ebb and flow of ancient seas,
Echo in the passing breeze.

Hushed Harbor Tales

Harbor's quiet, calm embrace,
Hides a thousand tales of grace.
Ships that rest and waves that dream,
In the harbor's tranquil seam.

Lighthouse sends its lonely beam,
Guarding whispers, silken stream.
Fisher's nets and anchors cast,
In the harbor's peaceful vast.

Muffled sounds of distant shores,
Blend with tales the harbor stores.
In the still and silent night,
Harbor's tales drift out of sight.

Murmuring Tides

Murmuring tides in twilight's hue,
Speak of secrets old and new.
Gentle waves in steady beat,
Caress the earth beneath our feet.

Echoes linger, soft and low,
Sharing tales of long ago.
Waters weave their ancient lore,
In the murmuring tides they pour.

From dawn's light to dusk's retreat,
Tides and whispers softly meet.
In their murmur, we confide,
Mysteries of the ocean wide.

Under the Gentle Swell

Beneath the skies where seagulls dwell,
Soft waves weave their magic spell.
Whispers of the ocean tell,
Secrets where the shadows fell.

Dolphins dance in silent streams,
Moonlight glows in silvery beams.
Stars above in distant dreams,
Blend with calm, serene themes.

Tides embrace in rhythmic flow,
Mysteries in depths below.
Ancient tales the gales bestow,
Songs of yesteryears they show.

Submerged Harmonies

In the heart of ocean's glow,
Melodies in currents flow.
Guardians of depth bestow,
Tunes from years so long ago.

Coral reefs in symphony,
Crafting notes in harmony.
Every wave a gentle plea,
Calling forth old memories.

Echoes drift through caverns wide,
In the blue, the songs reside.
Hidden worlds where dreams collide,
Evermore where notes abide.

Ballad of the Brine

Waves that crash on rocky shore,
Speak of tales, forgotten lore.
Songs of ships and men of yore,
Echo through the ocean's roar.

Fishermen with salt-kissed skin,
Sail where endless blue begin.
Heartfelt ballads rise within,
Chants of courage, deep and thin.

Wind and sea in chorus cry,
Underneath the azure sky.
Heritage that won't deny,
In the brine, their voices lie.

Sea's Voices

On the crest of waves they sing,
Essence of the ocean's ring.
Windy whispers ever cling,
To the tales the waters bring.

Mystic chants in every gale,
Spoken softly, never frail.
In the depths the words exhale,
Echoes of an ancient trail.

Salted spray and tides align,
Crafting stories so divine.
In the seas where voices shine,
Endless songs of the brine.

Lapping Lore

Waves that whisper, tales of yore,
Tidal rhythms, ancient roar.
Moonlit trails of pearly light,
Guide the sailors through the night.

Crabs that scuttle, shells that gleam,
Seaweed dances in a dream.
Shores that echo, songs unseen,
Nature's stories softly keen.

Tides that rise and gently fall,
Ebb and flow, a siren's call.
Whispers tell of distant lands,
Through the shells on grainy sands.

Hushed Horizons

Softly, softly speaks the dawn,
Spreading hues upon the lawn.
Morning mist, a veil so thin,
Daylight's whispers now begin.

Mountains standing tall and wise,
Catch the first light in their eyes.
Valleys wake and rivers hum,
Nature's chorus has begun.

Skies that stretch, so wide, so clear,
Hold the secrets, keep them near.
Peaceful, tranquil, breaks the day,
In hushed horizons, night gives way.

Secrets of the Swell

Beneath the waves, where secrets lie,
Hidden realms defy the sky.
Fishes dart in streams of light,
Colors bloom in depths of night.

Reef-bound whispers, corals sing,
Oceans cradle everything.
Deep below where shadows dance,
Ancient stories find their chance.

Currents carry tales untold,
Mysteries of blue and gold.
Every swell a secret keeps,
In the heart where silence sleeps.

Quiet Intertidal Tales

Between the tides where worlds collide,
Creatures roam and gulls reside.
Pools of life in rocky nooks,
Stories hidden in their looks.

Barnacles that cling so tight,
Witnessed time through day and night.
Anemones with colors bright,
Shelter life from hungry sight.

Rhythms of the ocean's song,
In quiet intertidal throng.
Nature's tales in whispers told,
In the ebb and flow, unfold.

Silence of the Swell

Waves whisper soft tales, otherworldly and bright,
In the haunting stillness of the star-pricked night.
Moonlight spills silver on the endless dark bay,
Where the silence of the swell sweeps visions away.

Breezes intertwine with the murmuring deep,
Secrets they cradle, with patience they keep.
Lost dreams are ferried on seafarer's breath,
In the hush of the ocean, the quiet of death.

Far on the horizon, ambitions dissolve,
In the tranquil embrace, mysteries evolve.
Tidal rhythms hum a formless, wild song,
Eternal, unyielding, where silence belongs.

Conversations with Coasts

Whispers of foam dance on golden shorelines,
Each wave's gentle call croons nuanced design.
Footprints are etched in the sand's fleeting script,
Where silken tides tell stories richly equipped.

Gulls herald the morning with jubilant cries,
Skies blush in response to dawn's tender sighs.
Pebbles converse in the surf's soft embrace,
Tracing the lineage of time's gentle pace.

Bones of the earth, where the land meets the sea,
Engage in a dialogue ancient and free.
Every shell, every stone holds tales untold,
A discourse of epochs where dreams unfold.

Ripples and Reveries

A pebble cast wide sends whispers around,
In ripples they wander, in dreams they'd be found.
Circles expanding in crystalline grace,
Echoes of moments in liquid embrace.

Reflections are twined with memories so bright,
Fragmented reveries captured in light.
Streams of existence flow endless and true,
Mirroring worlds both forgotten and new.

Surface bound gardens of shadow and gleam,
Subaqueous visions on the surface teem.
Ripples dissolve into whispers that die,
Only to be born anew in night sky.

Saltwater Secrets

In the depths of the azure, where sea serpents lie,
Hidden within currents, beneath a tethered sky.
There lie saltwater secrets, in brine they're kept,
Guardians of the deep, in silence they've slept.

Coral reefs whisper of ages gone by,
Of shipwrecks and treasures and long-lost cries.
The salt in the waves, preserving the lore,
Each droplet a chapter in ocean's grand score.

Sunlight descends through the watery cloak,
Illuminating secrets and words unspoke.
Delve into the waters, seek what they hold,
For the ocean's true heart remains untold.

Reflections in Ripples

In mirrored waves I see my face,
A silent echo of life's embrace,
Each ripple tells a tale untold,
In waters calm, my heart unfolds.

Shadows dance on liquid glass,
Moments fleeting, never last,
In stillness, whispers find their place,
A tranquil realm where dreams chaste.

Secrets hide beneath the sheen,
In waters dark, where I've been,
Ripples spread in circles wide,
Touching realms both far and nigh.

Moonlight's touch, a silver kiss,
In reflections, silent bliss,
Ripples fade yet leave a mark,
In the quiet, hearts embark.

Time captured in watery frames,
Life's choreographed, ephemeral games,
Reflections show what's passed us by,
In each ripple, a silent sigh.

Sounds of the Abyss

In the deep, where shadows play,
Echoes linger, night and day,
Songs emerge from fathoms low,
Melodies where darkness flows.

Whispers ride the ocean's breath,
Carried from realms between life and death,
Each note a tale of ancient lore,
Revealing secrets of the ocean floor.

Beneath the waves, the chorus hums,
Drawing life to unheard drums,
Rhythms pulse in currents cold,
Voices of the abyss are bold.

Stars above, and depths below,
Hear the call, the undertow,
Every creature hears its song,
In the abyss, where they belong.

Moon's glow filters twilight's kiss,
Connecting realms 'twixt dark and bliss,
In the depths, the notes persist,
Timeless sounds of the abyss.

Chants of the Current

Waves that dance in endless streams,
Whisper chants of ancient dreams,
Currents sing of journeys past,
In their flow, memories cast.

Wandering tides of sapphire hues,
Choral whispers, echoed muse,
In their song, the world unwinds,
Nature's voice, in currents, binds.

Songs of whales and distant cries,
Mixed with tales the sea denies,
Salt-kissed hymns of time and space,
In their ebb, we find our place.

Currents weave through realms unseen,
Chants of blue and emerald green,
From depths unknown to shores so near,
Their melodies, forever clear.

Ripples hum in gentle streams,
Carrying forth a sea of dreams,
In their chants, the world aligns,
Tales of old and future signs.

Silent Shores

On shores where silence meets the sea,
Whispers tell what words can't be,
Footprints trace a quiet path,
In sand and time, hearts find their bath.

Waves curl gently with a sigh,
Echoing the distant sky,
Here where silence softly swells,
In solitude, the spirit dwells.

Glistening sands by moonbeam kissed,
Hold secrets in a lover's tryst,
Silent shores, a sacred space,
Cradling dreams in tender grace.

Breezes soft, and shadows deep,
Where land and starlight secrets keep,
In the hush, we hear the more,
Silent tales on quiet shores.

Among the waves and silent air,
We find a peace beyond compare,
Where dreams and silence intertwine,
On quiet shores, our hearts align.

Coastal Dialogues

Waves converse with the weary sand,
Soft whispers of the moon's command.
Seagulls echo tales far and wide,
Breath of ocean, ebb and tide.

Driftwood carries messages old,
Secrets in the beach's fold.
Foam writes stories on the shore,
Calls the wanderer, explore.

Salt air lingers in the dusk,
Promising of treasure's husk.
Sun descends beneath the blue,
Night weaves dreams in sea's hue.

Subtle Sea Stories

Ripples trace a hidden lore,
Where echoes of the past adore.
Coral gardens bloom below,
In silent rhythms, secrets grow.

Shells sing soft, in gentle tones,
Of shipwrecks lost and sailors' moans.
Breezes carry tales untold,
Of mysteries in the ocean's hold.

Stars above and fish beneath,
Weave together sky and reef.
Tides recede to whisper low,
Stories only sea would know.

Murmurs Amid Mare

In the depths, where silence sleeps,
Whales' deep songs the darkness keeps.
Schools of silver dart and gleam,
Within the blue, a tranquil dream.

Beneath the waves, a dance of light,
Jellyfish in ghostly flight.
Anemones in colors bright,
Guard their homes, both day and night.

Currents carve a tale so grand,
Ancient voices from the sand.
In the stillness of the blue,
Murmurs whisper, always true.

Aquatic Hush

Dolphins leap in morning glow,
Through the quiet depths they go.
Sunbeams pierce the waters clear,
Bringing warmth to oceans dear.

Turtles glide in solemn grace,
Ancient wisdom on their face.
Every splash and wave's caress,
Mark the ocean's soft finesse.

From abyss to shore's embrace,
Nature's harmony we trace.
In the calm of sea's deep hush,
Life's true whispers gently rush.

Rhythms on the Horizon

The sun dips low with gentle ease,
In pastel hues, the sky does tease,
Each wave a rhythm in the breeze,
A dance of nature's melodies.

The horizon whispers tales unknown,
Of lands afar, where dreams have grown,
In twilight's hush, a seed is sown,
To wander forth, yet not alone.

Stars ignite as daylight fades,
Guiding hearts through twilight's shades,
In their light, a path is laid,
Where night and dreams serenade.

Echoes linger in the night,
Of day's end and morning's light,
In between, the world takes flight,
On wings of silence, pure and bright.

The moon ascends, a silver queen,
Her reflection, a tranquil sheen,
In her glow, the world is seen,
A rhythm on the horizon serene.

Melodies of the Mistral

Winds that dance through ancient trees,
Whisper tales on every breeze,
Nature's symphony with ease,
A melody that cannot cease.

Rustling leaves a gentle song,
Echoes where the heart belongs,
In the meadow, bold and strong,
The Mistral sings all day long.

Mountains hum in deep refrain,
Echoes float across the plain,
In this air, we break our chain,
Find a solace in the strain.

Valleys echo with the sound,
Nature's music all around,
In the Mistral, high and proud,
Every note is nature's crown.

As the twilight paints the sky,
Winds of change, they bid goodbye,
Yet their song will never die,
In the hearts where they reside.

A Murmur in the Moonlight

In the moonlight, shadows play,
Whispering secrets, night and day,
Stars above in grand array,
Murmurs in the dark convey.

Silver beams through branches weave,
Casting spells on all who believe,
In this light, our hearts perceive,
Dreams that night alone can weave.

Silent whispers in the air,
Linger on without a care,
In their solace, we find where,
Our deepest hopes and wishes fare.

The moon, a guardian from above,
Shines on secrets that we love,
In her glow, the stories shove,
A murmur in the night thereof.

As dawn approaches with its hue,
Moonlight fades but dreams stay true,
In the whispers, old and new,
A murmur left for me and you.

Seaside Soliloquy

Waves that kiss the sandy shore,
Tell old tales from days of yore,
In their rhythm, I explore,
Secrets of the ocean's core.

Seagulls cry above the foam,
Finding peace where waves do roam,
In their flight, my heart finds home,
Where the skies and seas are known.

Pebbles shimmering in the sand,
Stories held in every grain,
Each a part of nature's plan,
In the seaside's vast domain.

Sunsets paint the world in gold,
Every hue and shade unfold,
In this light, we're never old,
Seaside whispers soft and bold.

Night descends with stars so bright,
Reflecting in the ocean's might,
In their glow, our hearts unite,
Seaside soliloquy's delight.

Gentle Cadence

In the hush of twilight's grace,
Soft whispers fill the air,
A rhythm in the quiet space,
A melody beyond compare.

Footfalls echo soft and slow,
Through the meadows green,
Where the gentle rivers flow,
And night's calm can be seen.

Stars begin their silent song,
Glistening in the night,
They've danced this way for eons long,
In the tranquil, fading light.

Every leaf a lullaby,
Each breeze a soft refrain,
In the night's soft, tender sigh,
Nature's gentle cadence reigns.

Hearts attuned to whispered prayer,
In the night's embrace,
Find their solace and repair,
In gentle cadence, grace.

Conversations with the Sea

Waves that whisper tales untold,
Crash upon the sandy shore,
Secrets in their foamy fold,
Infinite, forevermore.

The ocean's voice, a timeless hymn,
Speaks of journeys vast and deep,
Of battles fought and whimsic dreams,
In waves that never sleep.

Shells that sing remembrance songs,
Of days beneath the brine,
Ghostly echoes all night long,
Structures of a bygone time.

Stars reflect on liquid glass,
Moonlight dances free,
In these moments that shall pass,
Conversations with the sea.

Salt and spray upon my face,
A dialogue so grand,
Nature's constant, gentle embrace,
Written in the shifting sand.

Vibrations of the Blue

Skies that hum a soothing tune,
Clouds that drift in peace,
Underneath the watchful moon,
Where all our troubles cease.

Ripples on a tranquil pond,
Echo out in waves,
Like whispers of a quiet bond,
That tenderly behaves.

In the sapphire vast expanse,
Winds sing soft and true,
Nature's timeless, lovely dance,
Vibrations of the blue.

Mountains standing tall and proud,
Shadows cast so long,
Beneath the sky, no longer loud,
In silence, nature's song.

Peaceful rhythms softly played,
In the air and sea,
Every note a woolen braid,
In blue's tranquility.

Sailing on Breathless Breezes

Canvas sails embrace the wind,
Silent as a whisper,
Cutting through the sapphire waves,
Gliding like a glister.

Dreams unfurl with every gust,
On seas of liquid glass,
Horizon's edge, a boundless trust,
In the future's silent clasp.

Star maps guide the voyage bold,
Where shadows dare not tread,
Through the calm and tempest cold,
By silent zephyrs led.

Wings of albatross inspire,
Grace in endless flight,
Breathless breezes lift us higher,
Into the velvet night.

Voyage ends in morning's glow,
Anchors kissed by dawn,
On shores where only dreamers go,
Breathless breezes gone.

Secrets Beneath the Surface

Beneath the sunlit waves they hide,
Secrets deep and grand,
Mysteries of oceanic stride,
Written in the sand.

Coral whispers legends old,
Of ships long lost to time,
In the silence, tales unfold,
Unheard by hearts sublime.

Mermaids guard the hidden pearls,
In caverns drenched in blue,
Songs of love and distant worlds,
Where echoes drown in dew.

Fish flash like living jewels,
In the emerald maze,
Guardians of the ancient pools,
In twilight's softest haze.

Silent currents weave the past,
In tides that never cease,
Secrets held and shadows cast,
In depths where dreams find peace.

Coastal Echoes

Whispers of the wind on sandy shores,
Gulls cry out, an endless score,
Waves collapse, a rhythmic roar,
In coastal echoes, forever more.

Footprints fade with each new tide,
Whispers linger, where dreams reside,
Seashell stories, heard far and wide,
By coastal echoes, time and tide.

Sunsets blaze in hues of gold,
Stories ancient and yet untold,
In the waves, the heart grows bold,
Echoes of the coast, both young and old.

The sea's embrace, a lover's sigh,
Under the vast and open sky,
Coastal echoes never die,
Their song remains as ages fly.

Muting the Pier

Beneath the stars, the pier lies still,
Waves lap soft, they always will,
Timbers creak with stories to spill,
In muting silence, a tranquil thrill.

Cloaked in shadows, night's embrace,
Moonlit paths, a gentle trace,
Silent whispers fill the space,
The pier holds time in a quiet place.

Ghostly echoes from days long gone,
Softly heard in twilight's song,
Murmurs of a time that lingers on,
In muted tones, the memories belong.

As dawn breaks with a silent light,
Shadows flee from the fading night,
The pier stands in morning's sight,
Muted whispers, soft and bright.

Breath of the Brine

Salty kisses from the sea,
Breezes whisper wild and free,
Tales of sailors lost to thee,
In the breath of brine, eternity.

Swaying grasses kiss the shore,
Songs of seagulls evermore,
Brine's embrace, an open door,
To ocean's lore and ancient core.

Golden sunsets paint the bay,
Tides roll in with gentle sway,
Breath of brine, both night and day,
Guiding lost hearts on their way.

In every wave, a heartbeat true,
Nature's breath, old yet new,
In the brine, horizons blue,
Life's sweet rhythm, ever in view.

Crescendo of Currents

Waves rise in serene display,
Under the moon's soft sway.
A symphony of night and sea,
Harmonies of wild, flowing free.

Tides dance with nature's ease,
Currents surge, the world to please.
Ocean's breath, a timeless song,
In depths where shadows belong.

Foam crowns each cresting wave,
Aquatic realms, secrets they save.
Echoes of ages lost in time,
Rhythms whispered in ancient rhyme.

Stars reflect on waters deep,
Dreams in motion, secrets keep.
Eternal flow, night's quiet chant,
A ballet under the moon's enchant.

Sunrise heralds dawn's embrace,
Currents in a tranquil race.
Day's light brushes past the shore,
Crescendo fades, but forever more.

Silent Tides

Beneath the sky, the ocean sighs,
Silent rhythms where mystery lies.
In moon's gentle, watchful gaze,
Waves whisper through foglike haze.

Shorelines etched in soft caress,
Ebbing tides' gentle press.
Night's embrace, a velvet touch,
In stillness speaks so much.

Whispers carried by the deep,
Secrets in the quiet sleep.
Nature's lullaby hums low,
In silent tides, their rhythms flow.

Golden sands await the dawn,
Where dreams in shadows drawn.
Murmurs lost to morning light,
Echoes of the tranquil night.

Peace resides in liquid blue,
In the silence, worlds anew.
Tides retreat to whisper lore,
A hush to greet the endless shore.

Sibilant Ebbs

Hushed whispers in twilight's fall,
Soft sirens to the soul they call.
Every ripple, a gentle plea,
Songs of the vast and deepened sea.

Waves retreat with subtle grace,
Leave etched memories in their place.
Softly stated, yet profound,
In sibilant ebbs, serenity found.

Veils of mist on quiet tides,
Where the spirit of the ocean hides.
Crystalline reflections gleam,
In each murmured, endless dream.

Silver threads of twilight's glow,
In the ebb, their stories flow.
Night's soft breath, a chorus leads,
To shores where every secret bleeds.

Morning breaks with whispered song,
Tides retreat, the night prolong.
In each gentle ebbing sigh,
Whispers of the ocean lie.

Whispered Waters

Soft murmurs on twilight seas,
Whispered waters, gentle breeze.
Every wave a quiet note,
In nature's symphony, they float.

Moonlit paths on liquid glass,
Reflections of the night they pass.
Stories told in silvered light,
Whispered waters through the night.

Echoes in the calmest deep,
Where ancient secrets softly seep.
Tales of old, in ripples' tale,
Whispers that the stars unveil.

Soft sighs of the ocean's song,
Where whispered waters belong.
Cradle of the night's embrace,
Eternal rhythms find their place.

Morning sun's first gentle gleam,
Wakes the world from night's dream.
Whispered waters, day resumes,
Silent hymns in dawn's perfumes.

Subaqueous Tales

Beneath the waves, where secrets lie,
In coral caves, where fish swim by,
A world unseen by human eyes,
Where ocean's wonders mesmerize.

In depths adorned with azure hue,
A dance of life, a hidden view,
Anemones with tentacles sway,
In silent currents, day by day.

Ancient wrecks, with stories old,
Their masts and beams now draped in gold,
Of treasure lost and battles fought,
In watery graves, forever caught.

Gliding rays and turtles slow,
Through kelp forests, they gently go,
A silent world beneath the gale,
Whispers of subaqueous tale.

The ocean's deep, a mystic ode,
Its secrets, in the darkness stowed,
With every wave, a story sails,
The eternal charm of subaqueous tales.

Silent Shores

Where land and sea in silence meet,
A sandy stretch, untrod by feet,
The call of gulls, the whispering breeze,
Nature's calm in moments seized.

A twilight sky of pastel hues,
Reflecting on the ocean's blues,
Soft waves that kiss the pebbled beach,
In gentle rhythm, a quiet speech.

Footprints fade in shifting sand,
A fleeting mark of roving band,
The silence holds a tranquil grace,
Echoes of a peaceful place.

As night descends with velvet cloak,
Stars above, their light evoke,
Upon the shore, a world revives,
In silent shores, true beauty thrives.

Moonlit waves that glisten bright,
Nature's canvas in soft light,
In quiet shores, the heart explores,
The timeless wonder of silent shores.

Sibilant Surf Tales

Whispers of the ocean breeze,
Through swaying palms and bending trees,
Each wave that breaks upon the sand,
A soft touch from a distant land.

The sibilant surf with tales to tell,
Of distant journeys, tempest swell,
In every crest, a secret shared,
Of ocean's might and beauty spared.

Seashells scattered on the strand,
Echoes of the ocean's hand,
In their spirals, stories bound,
Of deep blue depths where life is found.

Children's laughter, old men's sighs,
Mixed with the sea's eternal cries,
A symphony of life and lore,
Embraced by the sibilant shore.

In dawn's first light or sunset's blaze,
The whispered tales of ocean's ways,
Are carried far in gentle swells,
The endless hum of surf tales.

Harmonic Horizons

Where sky meets sea in seamless line,
A blend of hues, a grand design,
The horizon hums with colors bright,
A symphony of day's first light.

Birds on wing with morning grace,
Skim the surface, leave no trace,
A world that wakes in softest tones,
In harmonic whispers, nature's own.

Ships on distant waves do sail,
Guided by the evening's trail,
A path of gold, a morning's breath,
Towards the horizon's soft caress.

Sunset hues of orange and red,
Stories of the day retread,
In twilight's glow, the sky alights,
Harmonic tones of coming nights.

The realms of sea and sky unite,
In endless dance of day and night,
A tranquil blend of sights and sounds,
Harmonic horizons' boundless bounds.

Soft Murmurs of the Deep

In the vessel of midnight, calmness we seek,
Whispers of waves, soft murmurs of the deep,
Gentle as dreams where shadows reside,
Cradled by echoes that time won't deride.

Beneath star-strewn veils, where secrets align,
Softly the waters in lullabies find,
Mysteries deep in an infinite sweep,
Stars in reflection, celestial peep.

Night's tender grace on waters so blue,
Serenades sung where emotions construe,
Infinite murmur in the still of the night,
Whispers of solace in the softest light.

Moonlight's caress, the ocean beholds,
Tales of the ages in silence unfolds,
Soft murmurs echo, deep in their keep,
Stories entwined in the depth of sleep.

In the silence of dark, where reveries leap,
Softly they call, the souls they entreat,
Boundless horizons in secrets still steeped,
Whispers unravel in the deepness of sleep.

Harmony in the Mist

In dawn's tender light, the mist gently weaves,
Harmony's song on the breath of the leaves,
Whispers of morning, so subtle, so sweet,
Nature's own murmur, where hearts gently meet.

Veiled in soft gauze, the land comes to glow,
Wondrous symphony in the mist below,
Each note a pearl in the silence entwined,
Rhythms of peace in the dawn we find.

Fragrance of dew in the morning's embrace,
Softly it sings, a symphony's grace,
Each droplet a note in harmonious rhyme,
Captured in moments of stillness sublime.

Eyes closed to echoes, heart wide with the bliss,
Songs without words in the morning mist,
Nature's own hymn in the softest of keys,
Melodies linger, sweet as the breeze.

Awaken to whispers the dawn has conceived,
Harmony's touch in the mist received,
A song that is felt, in silence persists,
Melodies found in the heart of the mist.

Ebb and Flow of Unspoken Songs

By the shore where secrets long to be shared,
Ebb and flow of unspoken songs bared,
Tides carry whispers on the crest of waves,
Silent dirges in oceanic enclaves.

In the hush of twilight, the waters speak,
Ebb and flow of unspoken words seek,
Stories entwined in the dance of the sea,
Emotions unfurl, from silence set free.

In moon's gentle gaze, the tides softly hum,
Ebb and flow in a rhythmic strum,
Unspoken tales from deep currents arise,
Each wave a verse under starry skies.

The ocean's embrace, a hymn uncontained,
Ebb and flow where echoes are sustained,
Unvoiced verses in a watery sweep,
Guardians of secrets the deep waters keep.

In the solstice of night, the silence belongs,
Ebb and flow of unspoken songs,
Echoes from depths in a ceaseless refrain,
Whispering secrets again and again.

Voices of the Ocean

In the heart of the sea, where whispers reside,
Voices of the ocean on the moon's tide,
Gentle as zephyrs, yet endless and free,
Echoes in harmony, deep as the sea.

Each wave a whisper, a voice in the choir,
Resonance of ages in watery spire,
Songs of the sirens in liquid embrace,
Cadence of ocean in rhythmic grace.

Silent narrations of old maritime,
Voices of the ocean in timeless rhyme,
Currents convey in whispers so brief,
Melodies etched in the coral reef.

Tales spun in brine, where mysteries thrive,
Voices of the ocean forever alive,
Symphony found in the ceaseless roar,
Epics unraveled upon the shore.

In the depths of the night, the stories unfurl,
Voices of the ocean, in whispers they swirl,
Consonance lingered in waves' soft devotion,
Songs sung eternal, by the heart of the ocean.

Beneath the Blue Veil

Beneath the blue veil, calm and serene,
Whispers of secrets, never seen.
Oceans of dreams in tranquil deep,
Mysteries hidden, shadows sleep.

Soft waves dance with light's gentle grace,
Waves caress the moon's light embrace.
Stars shimmer, reflecting the night,
In the blue, fantasies take flight.

Silent symphony, a muted song,
Life below thrives, echoes prolong.
Depths hold stories, untold and bright,
In the silence, wisdom's delight.

Boundless and vast, the open sea,
Guarding its tales, wild and free.
Lost in the ebb, the flow, the reel,
Underneath, truth's heart we steal.

Timeless water's endless embrace,
Cradles time, in a fluid space.
Beneath the blue veil, secrets stay,
Forever, in blue's gentle sway.

Soft Echoes

Soft echoes drift through time's soft haze,
Caressing hearts in delicate ways.
Whispers of past, quiet and light,
Glide gently through the sleeping night.

Memories dance in the soft embrace,
In shadows etched by time's own trace.
Stories linger in muted tone,
In the quiet, not alone.

Voices heard in a silent breeze,
Lost in time's unyielding seas.
Soft echoes, a gentle guide,
Through the corridors, where hearts reside.

Faint whispers of laughter, pure,
Echoes of love that still endure.
In the stillness, the past ignites,
Glimmers of dreams, soft delights.

Soft echoes, tender and sweet,
In the silence, where time and hearts meet.
In the stillness, find what's true,
In soft echoes, past renew.

Unseen Utterances

Unseen utterances, whispered low,
Soft confessions, hidden glow.
Words unsaid, in hearts they lie,
Beneath the surface, they sigh.

Silence echoes what cannot be,
Uttered truths lost to the sea.
Invisible in daylight's glare,
In shadowed corners, secrets share.

Tender thoughts kept close in pain,
In unseen whispers, the soul's refrain.
Unspoken lines carve their place,
In the quiet, we find their trace.

Unseen utterances, faint and fair,
In the heart's hidden, sacred lair.
Words that souls alone might bear,
Carried on the softest air.

Invisible bonds that thread the night,
In stillness, hold each truth tight.
Unseen utterances, deep and pure,
In silent reverence, we endure.

Reverberations Along the Shore

Reverberations along the shore,
Echoing whispers of ancient lore.
Waves that crash in rhythmic beat,
Stories carried in their retreat.

The sea's voice in timeless song,
In every wave, tales belong.
Echoes that ride on the ocean's call,
Sweeping cove and rocky wall.

Whispers of yesteryears, soft they blend,
In water's memory, tales unbend.
Reverberations in the deep blue's core,
Echoes bound forevermore.

Gentle caress of tidal grace,
Waves that find their resting place.
In each ripple, in every sway,
Sea's embrace, night and day.

Reverberations along the shore,
Unseen voices, ancient roar.
In the ebb and flow, secrets lie,
Underneath, heart's quiet sigh.

The Deep's Dialogue

Beneath the surface, whispers low,
Dark abysses softly glow,
Silent tales of watery deep,
Secrets ancient oceans keep.

Fathoms down where shadows play,
Timeless echoes drift astray,
Speak in tongues of silt and moan,
Voices carved from coral stone.

Currents swirl in mystic dance,
Shimmering in moonlight's trance,
Livelihoods of silent plight,
In the deep's eternal night.

Undertow with quiet grace,
Caresses each hidden place,
Urging secrets to arise,
From the water's dark disguise.

Tranquil darkness, sacred vast,
Holds the whispers of the past,
In each wave and murmur low,
Deep's dialogue continues slow.

Sea's Sighs

Waves upon the shore do sing,
Stories that the sea does bring,
With their salty, briny breeze,
Secrets whispered through the seas.

Foam-kissed sands in dusk's retreat,
Echo footprints, fleeting, sweet,
As the sighing ocean sways,
Whispering of bygone days.

Soft laments of ships long gone,
Sailor's dreams and anchor's song,
Each drawn breath upon the tide,
Carries messages to hide.

Lighthouses with solemn beams,
Cast their gaze on silent streams,
Guiding lost and wandering souls,
Through the sea's unending shoals.

Eternal sighs, profound and deep,
Guard our secrets in their keep,
In each breath the ocean cries,
Hear the whispered sea's soft sighs.

Murmurs of the Ocean

Waves caress the sandy shore,
Softly murmuring evermore,
In the night, they tell their tale,
Of endless winds and fleeting sail.

Echoes linger in the deep,
Waters where the dreams do sleep,
Mystic murmurs, soft and kind,
In the ocean, secrets bind.

Crests of silver, crests of white,
Glimmer in the pale moonlight,
Songs of old and stories new,
Weave the ocean's gentle hue.

Drifting in their liquid song,
Carry whispered dreams along,
To the hearts that lie in wait,
For the ocean's whispered fate.

Whispers in the sea's embrace,
Hold the shadows in their place,
Endless murmurs, quiet and slow,
In the ocean's gentle flow.

Echoes of the Sea

In the echoes of the deep,
Silent promises do sweep,
Through the darkened, liquid halls,
Where the endless water falls.

Each new wave a story brings,
Of forgotten, quiet things,
In the sea's eternal play,
Whispers greet the dawning day.

Sunlight filters, gently casts,
On the ocean's moving vast,
Each reflection, rippling song,
Tales of where the waves belong.

Sea birds cry, their voices thin,
Mix with waves, where myths begin,
In their calls, the stories yearn,
To the ocean's depths, return.

Echoes in the briny deep,
Songs and stories, there to keep,
Endless as the vast expanse,
Sea's eternal echoing dance.

Oceanic Omens

Whispers linger in the tide,
Foretelling tales of far and wide.
Beneath the crest, the secrets speak,
Of oceans deep and futures bleak.

Moonlight dances on the wave,
A ghostly light in twilight's grave.
Beneath the surf, where shadows play,
Mysteries of night and day.

Glistening foam in moon's embrace,
Hints at magic's fleeting trace.
Voices rise as waters churn,
Destinies await their turn.

Currents weave a story's thread,
Binding dreams of future and dread.
From depths unknown, the omens rise,
Speaking truth beneath the skies.

Every ripple marks a sign,
In the ocean's grand design.
Tales of wonder and despair,
Flow through waves in open air.

Aqueous Enigmas

Ripples on a tranquil pond,
Reflecting mysteries far beyond.
The surface glimmers, secrets hold,
In liquid tales forever told.

With every splash, a riddle stirs,
Whispering truths like ancient slurs.
Hidden depths hold answers close,
In nature's enigmatic prose.

Reflections shimmer, truths obscure,
Beneath the calm, a world unsure.
Waves of wonder weave a spell,
In aqueous tales that oceans tell.

Bubbles rise with silent grace,
From shadowed depths of darkest place.
Each a puzzle, lost in time,
Echoes of an ancient rhyme.

Beneath the glassy, mirrored shield,
A hidden world is thus revealed.
In watery depths, enigmas wait,
For those who seek to know their fate.

Stillwater Secrets

In tranquil pools where silence reigns,
Lie whispered secrets, held in chains.
Still waters guard their tales so deep,
In mirrored depths, where shadows sleep.

Reflections dance on liquid glass,
A silent play as moments pass.
Beneath the calm, a hidden lore,
Sealed in stillness, evermore.

Leaves that float on surface clear,
Whisper secrets, soft and near.
In hush of dawn and quiet night,
Stillwater's secrets come to light.

Gently touched by morning breeze,
The water murmurs through the trees.
Ancient stories softly spill,
Where time stands whispering still.

In quietude, the pond reveals,
The silence that the heart conceals.
In tranquil depths, the secrets keep,
In stillwater's silent sweep.

Perpetual Murmurs

Eternal whispers of the sea,
A ceaseless, soft soliloquy.
In constant waves, the secrets blend,
With murmurs that will never end.

Each ebb and flow, a story told,
In ancient tongues, the waters hold.
The past and present intertwine,
In murmured sounds, a song divine.

Through day and night, the ocean speaks,
In murmurs soft, in roaring peaks.
Beneath the waves, a chorus sings,
Of timeless tides and endless springs.

The surf resounds with tales anew,
Of sunken ships and skies of blue.
In endless murmurs, strong and mild,
The ocean's voice both fierce and wild.

Forever shall the waters sway,
With murmurs that will never stray.
In every wave, a timeless lore,
The ocean whispers evermore.

Depths' Echoes

In twilight's grasp, the waters sigh,
Murmurs rise from caverns deep,
Ancient songs in whispers fly,
Mysteries in shadows seep.

Beneath the waves where secrets lie,
Dreams of old in currents spin,
Voices lost in ages high,
Echoes call from realms within.

Moonlight dances on the crest,
Rhythms chant in solitude,
Ocean's heart in silent quest,
Lullabies of amplitude.

Below the rage, below the roar,
Softly hums the sea's embrace,
Whispers woven evermore,
In depth's echoing grace.

From abyss to surface bright,
Hidden tales through waters flow,
Echoes whisper through the night,
Seeking hearts that long to know.

Seaward Soliloquies

Beneath the sky where seagulls roam,
Echoes merge with winds so free,
Whispers rise in frothy foam,
Lamentations of the sea.

Soft soliloquies they weave,
Ancient tongues in tides' refrain,
Seaward songs at dusk and eve,
Waves that speak of joy and pain.

Sunset's glow on waters pure,
Murals painted, stories told,
Silent verses that endure,
In every wave, a saga bold.

Through the mists and through the haze,
Voices call from yonder shore,
Odes to lost and bygone days,
Resonance forevermore.

Ebb and flow in rhythmic glide,
Passing secrets lost in glee,
Tell the tales the waters hide,
In their seaward soliloquy.

Soundless Shores

In the hush of morning light,
Waves roll in with silent grace,
Whispers form from misty night,
Ancient echoes find their place.

Footsteps fade on silver sands,
Ephemeral as dreams of yore,
Time slips through unseen hands,
In the realm of soundless shore.

Moonlit paths on tranquil sea,
Shadows drift in pure embrace,
Where the sky and water meet,
Silent worlds in sacred space.

Gentle breezes, sweet caress,
Melodies without a sound,
Touch the heart with soft finesse,
In these shores that love surrounds.

Far away from tempest's call,
Lies a haven, peace restores,
In the quiet, hear it all,
Life's heartbeat on soundless shores.

Sentient Seas

In the night, the waters gleam,
Stars reflect their silver light,
Oceans weave a sentient dream,
Breathing in the silent night.

Currents pulse with life unseen,
Energy of ancient lore,
Sentient seas in sapphire sheen,
Mysteries forevermore.

Tides converse with moon's caress,
Shifting sands in whispered dance,
Waves reveal and waves suppress,
In their boundless, vast expanse.

Life within the depths profound,
Teeming worlds in liquid grace,
Every ripple, every sound,
Holds the universe's face.

From abyssal plains to shore,
Seas perceive with mindful eyes,
Sentient, eternal, evermore,
Bearing witness, seer's eyes.

Marine Meditations

Beneath the waves, where silence reigns,
A world unfolds, untouched by pains.
Coral castles, colors bright,
Guardians of the deep, in endless night.

Whales serenade with ancient songs,
Echoes where vast mystery belongs.
Schools of fish in synchronized dance,
Life in the blue, a trance, a chance.

Shimmering scales in sunbeam's kiss,
A tranquil world bathed in bliss.
Untamed currents sweep and sway,
Dreamlike scenes in pure ballet.

Seashell whispers secrets old,
In sandy beds, stories told.
Crabs in crevices, hidden and shy,
Life unfolds where depths comply.

Surface breaks as dolphins leap,
Guardians of the ocean's keep.
Meditative, the sea's embrace,
Eternal calm in nature's grace.

Ethereal Edges

Glimmers dance on twilight's veil,
In transient moments, truths unveil.
Stars emerge in quiet grace,
Mapping skies in celestial lace.

Wisps of light in astral streams,
Guide the night through endless dreams.
Horizon kissed by moon's soft glow,
Ethereal edges, far below.

Guardian spirits in shadows play,
Silent watchers through the fray.
Mystic pathways, unseen threads,
In whispers spoke, all fear sheds.

Time distorts in twilight's grasp,
Hold of night, a gentle clasp.
Whispers of old in winds entwine,
Secrets of space, on hearts enshrined.

Eternal twilight, ever serene,
Bridging worlds in realms unseen.
Edge of dreams where reality bends,
Journey infinite, with no ends.

Sonic Surf Stories

Waves crash in rhythmic beat,
Nature's song, a tale complete.
Tides that whisper, tales untold,
Ancient stories in swells unfold.

Seabirds call in early morn,
In golden light, day is born.
Sonic echoes, a mystic lore,
Shoreline secrets, heart's implore.

Surfing souls ride liquid paths,
In symphony, the ocean laughs.
Board meets wave in fluent dance,
Moments merge in vibrant trance.

Gull cries mix with crashing foam,
By the sea, the heart finds home.
Melodies of waves inspire,
Sonic tales of pure desire.

Sunset cloaks in glowing hues,
A canvas painted in ocean blues.
Harmony in each wave's sigh,
Stories of surf beneath the sky.

Rippled Reflections

Lakeside calm, a mirror clear,
Reflections ripple, drawing near.
Mountains echo in water's face,
Nature's portrait in soft embrace.

Soft winds brush the water's skin,
Whispered tales of where we've been.
Clouds drift by in mirrored sheen,
Echoed dreams, serene and keen.

Twilight's touch on liquid glass,
Moments frozen, time can't pass.
Reflections bend in dappled light,
Ripples dance in fading sight.

Stars align in mirrored frames,
Silent echoes of whispered names.
Ripples tell of endless ties,
Reflected worlds in night's guise.

Stillness speaks in gentle tones,
Symphony in water's own.
Reflections ripple, tales unfold,
Whispers of a world retold.

Caresses of the Sea

Soft whispers glide on twilight's breeze,
In ocean's arms, our troubles cease.
Waves gently kiss the sandy shore,
Nature's embrace, forever more.

Stars reflect in waters deep,
Cradled in dreams that never sleep.
Moonlight dances on waves so free,
In the caresses of the sea.

Beneath the tide, secrets reside,
Mysteries the ocean cannot hide.
Silent melodies, ancient and wise,
Sing to the heart, under moonlit skies.

Footprints fade, a transient mark,
Under a canopy dark.
Yet memory lingers, whispering true,
The sea's caresses, always renew.

Subtle Serenades

Beneath the canopy of night,
Soft serenades take flight.
Whispers of leaves in gentle sway,
A night's promise, till break of day.

Crickets play their timeless tune,
Harmonizing with the moon.
Stars blink in rhythmic delight,
Crafting dreams in silent night.

Wind brushes past in soft embrace,
Singing secrets with gentle grace.
Each note a touch, unseen yet true,
Serenades in a world of blue.

In twilight's arms, peace is found,
With every subtle, soothing sound.
Silent whispers, nature's own,
A symphony of the unknown.

Ripples of Silence

In the stillness, ripples spread,
Words unspoken softly said.
Tranquil waters, mirror clear,
Reflecting all that we hold dear.

A stone cast in, gentle arc,
Silent echoes in the dark.
Waves expand, a tender sigh,
As silence sings a lullaby.

Moon above, with watchful eye,
Witnesses as moments fly.
Ripples tell of times gone by,
Of whispered dreams and muted cries.

In quietude, truth is found,
In ripples' soft and gentle sound.
Silence speaks in waves so slow,
What hearts conceal, the waters show.

Hidden Melodies

In the forest, hidden deep,
Melodies awaken from their sleep.
Notes entwine with rustling leaves,
A hidden song the heart perceives.

Birds sing tales of days gone by,
Choruses that lift the eye.
Streams hum softly to the land,
Nature's orchestra at hand.

Whispers of the wind conspire,
Adding depth to nature's choir.
In the quiet, secrets lie,
Melodies hidden in the sky.

Hear the symphony, soft and true,
With every step, a note renews.
Hidden melodies burst to life,
In the heart of the forest's quiet strife.

Seaside Secrets

Whispers in the waves, so light,
Tales of moonlit, silent nights.
Seashells hold the past in sleep,
Oceans in their secrets, deep.

Foamy crests that kiss the shore,
Guard the dreams of sailors, lore.
Stars reflected in the tide,
Where the mermaids used to hide.

Winds that sing in unison,
With each ray of rising sun.
Hidden treasures in the sand,
Grains that slip right through your hand.

Seagulls trace the azure sky,
Echoes where the oceans sigh.
Footprints vanish, left with care,
Secrets with the salt-filled air.

Calm before the storm's embrace,
Nature's whispers, light and grace.
Veil of mist on morning's call,
Shrouds the beach, enchanting all.

Shoreline Serenade

Glistening at the brink of dawn,
Footprints mark where love is drawn.
Tender touch of waking light,
Greets the boundless ocean's might.

Symphony of waves and breeze,
Notes that drift upon the seas.
Harmonies that gulls compose,
Dance where water, sand repose.

Silhouette of distant sails,
Stories told by wind that wails.
Sunset drapes in hues so grand,
Painting dreams upon the sand.

Echoes where the twilight sings,
Touch of night with unseen wings.
Rhythms of the tide align,
Serenade, the day's decline.

Candles of the stars ignite,
Guiding thoughts through softest night.
Shoreline's song that fades so slow,
Lingers 'til dawn's morning glow.

Ocean's Quiet Call

Beneath the surface, calm and clear,
Echoes linger, none can hear.
Soft the call of ocean's song,
Timeless, gentle, lasting long.

Moon reflects its silver hue,
On the waters, dark and blue.
Currents weave their silent tales,
Through the deeps, where peace prevails.

Hidden depths where secrets lie,
Unknown truths beneath the sky.
Coral gardens, vibrant, bright,
In the day or through the night.

Ships that drift on lazy tides,
Seek out whispers ocean hides.
Songs of distant, far-off lands,
Lulled within the waves' commands.

Shores that cradle ocean's edge,
Hold the quiet, whispered pledge.
Ancient voice that softly speaks,
Fills the night and calmer creeks.

Rippling Confessions

Secrets speak in waters deep,
In the ripple's gentle sweep.
From the hearts of ocean's hold,
Mysteries, in whispers told.

Pebbles thrown in playful glee,
Spread their tales for all to see.
Circles grow and fade from view,
Every wave a story new.

Light that dances, gleams and sways,
Moves with currents, sea's ballet.
Sunlight kissed and shadowed fears,
Merge within the tide's own tears.

Silent night and restless wave,
Confessions of the hearts that brave.
Tides that wash away the past,
Whispered truths that ever last.

Moon and stars in night's caress,
Hold the dreams and words confessed.
Rippling through the time's expanse,
Oceans' truth in endless dance.

Harmony of the High Seas

On waves that kiss the golden shore,
Caressed by winds, they gently pour,
The salty spray, a soft encore,
As seagulls sing and oceans roar.

Beneath the stars, the sailors dream,
Of lands afar and ancient gleam,
Their hearts aligned with nature's seam,
In rhythmic pulse, a soothing theme.

The moonlight dances on the tide,
In her embrace, the secrets bide,
A silken path, so smoothly slide,
Where night and ocean both confide.

The whales call out in echoed song,
With melodies both sweet and strong,
To distant ports where they belong,
A harmony that drifts along.

Embrace the peace the sea bestows,
In every peak and trough, it shows,
A tranquil heart in ebb and flows,
Where unity forever grows.

Breezy Confessions

Whispers float on twilight air,
Of secrets shared without a care,
The willow bows with tender flair,
Confessions soft, beyond compare.

Sunset hues in skies to blend,
In shadows where the branches bend,
A gentle breeze, the message sends,
Of truths the day can now amend.

Leaves do flutter, words unseen,
In every pause and space between,
A tale of love, both pure and keen,
With whispers from the evergreen.

The night's embrace, a calming shroud,
Where stars recount the words aloud,
In twinkling prose, so subtly proud,
Each hidden vow, they will endow.

Through every gust, a silent plea,
Of hearts that yearn to wander free,
In breezy strokes, their destiny,
A dance of whispered honesty.

Calm Currents

The river flows with quiet grace,
A mirror of the sky's embrace,
In gentle curves, it finds its place,
A seamless path, a tranquil space.

Beneath its surface, life does glide,
In shadows where the fish reside,
With nature's bounty as their guide,
In currents where all doubts subside.

The willows dip their branches low,
In reverence to the softest flow,
A harmony the waters know,
That into night and dreams will grow.

With pebbles smooth and stories old,
Of eras past and tales retold,
In every ripple, pure and bold,
A legacy the depths unfold.

So let the calmness fill your soul,
As waters of the river roll,
In endless streams that make you whole,
A life's journey to console.

Invisible Chants

In shadows deep where silence creeps,
Echoes of the past it keeps,
A melody through time it seeps,
In whispered tones, the forest weeps.

The moonlight casts a ghostly veil,
Where tales of old on winds do sail,
Invisible, yet not so frail,
In every breath, a haunting trail.

The stars converse in secret codes,
Above the night's deserted roads,
With ancient chants, the dark forebodes,
A harmony that seen forbodes.

Through hidden groves, the voices blend,
In timbered song they each defend,
In layered verse, they find a friend,
Invisible, yet they transcend.

A symphony beyond the sight,
In shadows, whispers claim the night,
With silent words that feel so right,
Invisible chants take their flight.

Lingering Notes of the Coast

The waves play tunes on pebbled shore,
Whispers of ancient, salt-sewn lore.
Seagulls' cries weave through the air,
Nature's choir, a song laid bare.

Footprints fade in shifting sand,
Ephemeral marks of an unseen hand.
Shells glisten, treasures cast,
Echoes of a time that's passed.

Sunset flames ignite the sky,
As day bids a soft goodbye.
Breath of brine fills the night,
Stars awaken, casting light.

In the cool and silent hours,
The coast reveals its hidden powers.
Dreams are born of ocean's kiss,
In this realm of tranquil bliss.

Morning dawns, the cycle starts,
Waves engage in ocean's arts.
Life persists in ceaseless flow,
Lingering notes of the coast bestow.

Tales from the Tide

Mystery lies in shifting sands,
Crafted by time's own careful hands.
Veiled stories etched by waves,
In watery tombs and secret caves.

Ships that sailed and men that roamed,
Found their peace where ocean foamed.
Barnacles cling to sunken wood,
Legends buried where they stood.

In the hush of twilight gray,
Tides recount what winds convey.
Ebb and flow, a whispering tune,
Chanting secrets to the moon.

In shells we hear the ocean's song,
A melody that's aged and strong.
Each tide a chapter to be read,
Written by currents, never dead.

The sea, a bard of endless prose,
Sings where only sailors go.
Tales from the tide, an endless dance,
Of nature's rhythm and happenstance.

Siren's Breath

A melody within the breeze,
Carries whispers across the seas.
Siren's breath in misty veil,
Calls to hearts with haunting wail.

In moonlit nights, their voices rise,
Soft and sweet, yet full of lies.
Luring souls with honeyed tones,
To coral beds and sailor's stones.

Glistening scales and eyes so deep,
Pledge promises they cannot keep.
Waves their playground, tides their song,
Echoes where the lost belong.

Beware the call of ocean's muse,
For it's a fate one cannot choose.
Her lullaby of false delight,
Leads astray in darkest night.

Siren's breath, a fleeting breeze,
A mortal's whisper lost at sea.
In her arms, both cold and warm,
Lie mysteries of tranquil storm.

Floating Memories

Tiny boats in harbor float,
Memory's vessel, love's small note.
Each wave a page of journeys past,
Echoed dreams by breezes cast.

Ripples tell of long-gone days,
In silent, reflective gaze.
Anchored tales in hearts survive,
Floating memories kept alive.

Mornings kiss the sea's cool face,
Awakening time's gentle grace.
Whispers of a life once led,
Faded footprints, words unsaid.

Evening paints the sky in gold,
Stories new and stories old.
In the hush of dusk's embrace,
Memories float to find their place.

Twilight's song and moonshine bright,
Guard these whispers of the night.
Floating memories drift and weave,
Tales of love we never leave.

Resonance of Waves

Whispers in the depths, an ancient song.
Echos of the sea where souls belong.
Rhythms pulse in time, the oceans' might.
In the dark of night, the stars shine bright.

Thunderous cries and call of distant shores.
Kingdoms of the deep, where water roars.
Voices rise and fall with each tide's crest,
Eternal dance, a sailor's heart at rest.

Silent symphony beneath the sky,
Sirens' calls that never say goodbye.
In the endless blue, the secret breath,
Mysteries of old, love's endless depth.

Tidal waves bring echoes from afar,
Melodies of ages, guiding star.
Harmony of seas, our spirits lave,
Lost within the resonance of waves.

Quiescent Coastlines

Silent shores where footfalls find retreat,
Sands embrace the earth beneath our feet.
Whispered breezes weave through ancient dunes,
Songs of twilight meet the night's soft tunes.

Lighthouses stand guard with endless gaze,
Guiding souls through mist and ocean's maze.
Stillness of the coast awash in light,
Breathing in the peace of endless night.

Salt and sea entwine in fragrant air,
Quiescent coastlines, beauty rare.
Starry skies reflect on waters calm,
Holding secrets in their tranquil palm.

Moonlit paths on waves that softly crest,
Nature's rhythm sings us into rest.
Gentle tides and nights where dreams align,
Quiescent coastlines, peace so divine.

Undertow Murmurs

Hidden currents twist beneath the sea,
Mysteries that pull so quietly.
Whispers of the deep, where shadows play,
Guiding us towards the breaking day.

Silent forces pull beneath the waves,
Darkened realms where silence freely paves.
Rhythms of the ocean's secret flow,
In the undertow, the mysteries grow.

Call of the unknown from deep below,
Murmurs of the tide that ebb and flow.
Currents guide the heart to hidden grooves,
Where the ocean's old and sacred moves.

Beneath the surface, life in subtle shifts,
Souls entwined in undertow's soft drifts.
Silent ballet of the deep unknown,
Undertow murmurs, ancient secrets shown.

Phantom Ocean Sounds

Echoes in the mist, where waves collide,
Phantom murmurs call from oceans wide.
Lost in time yet whispered through the breeze,
Haunting notes through ever-moving seas.

Songs of sirens long since swept away,
Lingering in the tides' eternal sway.
Phantoms of the past on waves resound,
In the ocean's voice their songs are found.

Deep within the ocean's hidden heart,
Melodies that never truly part.
Ghostly notes in foam and crashing spray,
Phantom voices in the ocean's play.

Eternal rhythms play on endless sands,
Guiding the lost with unseen hands.
In the ocean's voice, a tale retold,
Phantom ocean sounds both young and old.

Melancholy Shores

Upon the sands where dreams do fade,
Bleak horizons softly laid.
Whispers in the moonlight air,
Echoes of a love laid bare.

Gulls cry out in mournful tones,
Oceans pull at silent stones.
Footsteps lost in shifting tides,
Lonely hearts where sorrow bides.

Stars above in muted glow,
Cast their light on waves below.
Yet the stillness, cold and deep,
Guard the secrets they must keep.

Twilight sinks in shades of gray,
Scarred by memories' silent fray.
Silent waters, somber plea,
Masked beneath the endless sea.

A lonesome breeze through crooked trees,
Tells of pasts and tragedies.
Melancholy shores remain,
Carrying the soul's refrain.

Subterranean Stories

Deep within the earth's embrace,
Lies a world of endless grace.
Hidden tales in darkened halls,
Carved in stone by nature's calls.

Caverns whisper ancient lore,
Echoes of a time before.
Stalactites like tears of old,
Guard the secrets never told.

Rivers speak in shadowed tongues,
Silent songs forever sung.
Luminous in darkness bloom,
Life within the veiled gloom.

Crystal chambers, gemstone light,
Shimmer in the endless night.
Labyrinths of time unbound,
Stories in the silence found.

Mysteries through ages wove,
In the heart of earth's deep cove.
Subterranean stories lie,
Waiting 'neath the endless sky.

Calm Currents

Gentle waves caress the shore,
Softly whispering evermore.
Harmonies the ocean weaves,
In the dance of drifting leaves.

Sunlight glimmers on the crest,
Cradling waters now at rest.
Seagulls ride the tranquil air,
Peaceful moments everywhere.

Shoreline secrets softly kept,
In the tide where dreams have slept.
Every ripple, every seam,
Part of nature's gentle theme.

Azure skies above unfold,
Stories in the ripples told.
Beneath the gaze of endless blue,
Currents calm and ever true.

Silent symphony of grace,
Found in ocean's warm embrace.
Calm currents hold a timeless spell,
In their whisper, all is well.

Subtle Wave-Speak

Waves upon the shoreline break,
With a voice that whispers, wake.
Laughter in the foamy crest,
Whispers of the ocean's jest.

Secrets carried in the tide,
Murmurs from the oceanside.
Every wave a tale to tell,
Echoes in the rising swell.

Silent rhythms, ebb and flow,
Subtle voice the waters know.
In the dance of moonlit tide,
Gentle truths the waves confide.

Shoreline sings in tones subdued,
Beneath the sky of changing hues.
Mysteries in waves concealed,
Only to the heart revealed.

Subtle wave-speak, soft and light,
Songs of day and dreams of night.
In the ebb and flow we find,
Whispers of the ocean's mind.

Waveless Whispers

In the stillness of the ocean's hush,
Whispers ripple without a flush.
Secrets held in waters deep,
Guarded in eternal sleep.

Corals glimmer, soft and shy,
Underneath the tranquil sky.
Echoes of the silent tide,
Where moon and stars confide.

Mysteries of sunken ships,
Waveless whispers on their lips.
Timeless tales in shadows swirl,
Of lost sailors, sinuous whirl.

Quiet holds the ocean's breath,
Silent songs of life and death.
Waveless whispers gently speak,
In the heart of night so sleek.

Crystal waters, fathomless blue,
Carry whispers soft and true.
Secrets of the deep remain,
In waveless whispers' sweet refrain.

Auguries of Atlantis

Beneath the waves, where legends lie,
Atlantis dreams beneath the sky.
Prophecies in currents told,
Of a city draped in gold.

Meridian days and silver nights,
Visions glow in watery lights.
Stones inscribed with runes old,
Speak of tales yet untold.

Echos of the ancients' call,
In the sea's secretive sprawl.
Sunken halls and toppled spires,
Whispering of lost empires.

Rippled shadows, looming grand,
Guard the truths of fabled land.
In their depths, the auguries play,
Of Atlantis' bygone day.

Blue oracles, silent spheres,
Hold the wisdom, stilled with years.
In Atlantis' buried grace,
The auguries find their place.

Beneath the Brine

Beneath the brine, the world unfolds,
Mysteries of darkened folds.
Creatures glide in silent flight,
In realms of endless night.

Shadows dance in twilight beams,
Whispering ancient turtle's dreams.
Far below the surface sheen,
Secrets stir in silt unseen.

Coral castles, gardens wild,
Nature's wonders, undefiled.
In the deep where colors bloom,
A surreal and tranquil room.

Ancient treasures, lost in time,
Rest within the ocean's rhyme.
Jewels and gold, now ocean's claim,
Beneath the brine, they find no fame.

Eternal dances, currents weave,
Songs of sea the hearts believe.
Beneath the brine, a mystic trance,
Leaves the soul in silent dance.

Sunken Solitude

In the depths of endless night,
Solitude takes gentle flight.
Sunken echoes, soft and still,
Whisper through the ocean's chill.

Shadowed pathways, lost and old,
Silent stories, faintly told.
Wandering thoughts on currents ride,
In the solitude they bide.

Watery cloisters, calm and old,
Guard the secrets they behold.
Quiet realms where time stands still,
In the heart of ocean's will.

Ghostly ships in spectral rows,
In the deep where silence slows.
Echoes of a distant song,
In sunken solitude prolong.

Peaceful whispers, gentle tide,
Where the deepest dreams reside.
In the calm of ocean's grace,
Find in solitude your place.

Milton Keynes UK
Ingram Content Group UK Ltd.
UKHW020054270724
446062UK00003B/55

9 789916 763681